MY IRIDESCENT DAGGERS

Poems

Calista Ashmore

My Iridescent Daggers

Copyright © 2025 by Calista Ashmore

All rights reserved

No part of this publication may be reproduced, distributed, or transmitted in any form or by any means, including photocopying, recording, or other electronic or mechanical methods, without the prior written permission of the publisher, except in the case of brief quotations embodied in critical reviews and certain other noncommercial uses permitted by copyright law.

Printed in the United States of America

First Edition

Manufacturing by Lightning Source

Book Design by Necula Ioana Irina

Names: Ashmore, Calista, author.

Title: My Iridescent Daggers: Poems by Calista Ashmore

Identifiers: ISBN 9798992592733 - *(Hardcover)*

For all my homes—from back porches to brown eyes.

Contents

I Am From 1

Scorpio Moon 3

Estoy Lista 5

Dissociation 7

I Want to be Angry Enough for Revenge 11

Life As a Lasso 13

Laced with Outlaw 15

Tongue-Tied 17

Follow Me 19

Ranch Recital 21

The First Time I Saw My Father Cry 23

Star-Crossed 25

Of Your Jaguar Mouth 27

When My Mother Became a Grandmother 29

Oh, To Be a Maiden 31

Christian 33

Branded by an Indian Paintbrush 35

86 37

Forgiveness Trickery 39

Praying From a Sailboat, Maine. 41

Growing Pains 43

I Left the Light On 45

Fifteen	47
So, You Think You're a Black Kettle?	49
Castell, Texas	51
This Is the Last Poem I Write About You	53
Lay Your Head Where You Forget Your Fear	55
Witness	57
Stained	59
Sisters, Not Twins	61
The Third Parent & The Middle Child	63
Has Anybody Seen Mary Margaret?	65
LANDMAN	67
Belonging	69
I'm Planting	71
Del Rio	73
He Can Always Hear Me	75
Morning Melody	77
I Met Calista on a Park Bench	79
Good Luck	83
Nana's Chocolate Fudge (Serves You Right)	85
68	87
The First Time I Heard My Mother Cry	89
Acknowledgements	91

My Iridescent Daggers

I Am From

Red dirt stains my teeth and I sport it
like fine red wine

I am from pumpjack and jackrabbit
I am from stolen man's land
merciless
veiled with meandering cattle
I don't find the big cities much different

I am from vacant mesas
where boots host bottles
where hats are hooked

I am from high school sweethearts
in the land of broken hearts
as love here often ends
where a well-watered pasture begins
but I am from fidelity and something blue
I am from loyal vows and something used

I am from snake rattles and horse saddles
loot buried into the side of Packsaddle

I am from Velveeta and Rotel
I am from snuff-filled lips
I am from holster-clipped hips

Calista Ashmore

I am from bottom-shelf booze
too many loved ones used as a noose

I am from sunburnt gizzards
I am from flesh-colored blizzards

I am from rust-covered pliers
pulling loose teeth
I am from stickers and thorns
penetrating my feet

I am from square-toe gator
I am from first pew posture
I am from crossed T's and dotted I's

Where I am from
hogtied me
as I drove my guzzler
never crossing state lines
into the parallel sun

Scorpio Moon

I pucker up for crushed
velvet couch confessions
under match-stricken afterglow
sterile moonlight
haunted by midnight sirens
the scrapes of a seasoned record
the crashes of melting ice and herbal
liquor avalanching lips
spilling secrets onto
my ecclesiastic lap until the
blue dayspring birds
interrupt with song

Come into my living room
treat it as if a wooden screen
lives between our expressions and I have
dedicated my life to confidentiality
my black gown a uniform
rather than a silk dreaming suit,
anointing your sickness with Ophir—
I am celibate for the love of having
our innermost saints dance next to
the credenza while we sit and whisper
pitying the sinless soundly
sleeping at these hours

Calista Ashmore

Estoy Lista

My inheritance was given in full: cedar chest earth and faded citron agave. The dehydrated live oaks curve like the back of the neighbor's matted mule, that sweet meanderer, once as silver as an April morning. He would greet me with ease, beige hay hanging from his slippery, stiffened upper lip. While sipping my sorrow-stained coffee, perched on my grandmother's stripped peach-painted porch, I wonder if the cactus in the yard ever longs to be chartreuse. If it resents fate, planted only to be spotted with iridescent daggers. If it would dare uproot itself for the kaleidoscope city.

Calista Ashmore

Dissociation

I have found myself in an itchy spot
no longer complacent—shamefully obedient

holding down words until I choke on
ones that dig their nails into my throat
defying the swallowing of defiance
a sting that makes my eyes water
but I know will make my stomach hurt worse

Some call it
the prison of the mind
I must have Stockholm Syndrome
I'm crawling into the deep depths of my inner
willing my physical form to dissipate
fade at least
until I am sent into the damnation
that is my conscience
and I am nothing more

remove my legs

my fingers

my arm hair

leave me in my captivation
lose the key

I wonder if ghosts have the opportunity
to communicate with trees
the living and the late

both mute but not emotionless

draping and gaping silent
mouths over our every mistake
begging the wind to offer them
a powerful inhale to scream

I want to drown in my own judgements
as I hold my breath
completely immersed in
memories and
useless ideas
I wait
praying nobody taps my shoulder

I always tend to make bail
as with every
whisper
slamming door
snapping pencil tip
coffee drip
I come back
resurfacing
with a key on my lap

My Iridescent Daggers

legs

                       fingers

                                         arm hair

still intact.

Calista Ashmore

My Iridescent Daggers

I Want to be Angry Enough for Revenge

I want every pill they ingest over the next ten years
to be stamped with my initials
I want to be brave enough
with my chest puffed
like springtime eye bags
I want all birds to fly
like a mother with a problem child
in need of one more reason to evict
I want to stride down cobblestone
in six-inch stilettos
I want bystanders to whisper
that one has no Achilles heel
I want to be the reason they turn
their glass houses upside down
searching for the missing puzzle piece
the one the dog ate behind the sofa
I want an evil eye carved
into the trunk of an aspen tree
to wink as I walk by
I want the town to gossip
I remember that name, I remember that face, but I can't
remember her voice
I want them paranoid
I want to be the dancing man in their peripheral
I want to be the rotten peyote they swallowed
like Russian caviar
I want to be the dust of their kicked rocks
settling under their Persians
I want to expect nothing of them
I want to be angry
and them deserving
enough for revenge

Calista Ashmore

Life as a Lasso

I wrap and tie a big bow
around everything I've known
unwilling to let go
I am the noose and the target

I'll carry the weight behind me
swathe a handful of belongings
strap to the end with ribbon
and drag it while I leave home
I am the rope and the burn

Any who have confessed
love wanders my yard
sporting a cowhide necklace
I am the designer and the pawn shop

They attempt to run
while I charge forward
I never miss, never throw twice

I am not a disease, am not a bullet
just a flimsy and frayed little lasso
holding on for dear life

Calista Ashmore

Laced with Outlaw

Blackie and Webb, sheriffs
>kept the drunkards from bar brawls
>every Christmas Eve in West Texas

Lyons and James, ranchers
>average folk destroyed the land
>whilst they cared for it in North Texas

I am laced with outlaw
>a life of drawing white beans
>from an ixtle basket

I am laced with outlaw
>shootouts with engraved pistols
>bedroll caskets

I am laced with outlaw
>menudo and ceviche
>tongue stew

I am laced with Outlaw
>Tony Orlando
>Tony Lama

I am laced with outlaw
>a kerchief mutes my twang
>handmade stampede strings

I am laced with outlaw
>I can speak with animals
>a whistle and name

Calista Ashmore

I am the Sheriffs' great-granddaughter
        the ranchers' too

We roam while waiting on the silhouettes
        to guide us with the rusty flare stack hues

Tongue-Tied

I never wanted to taste the blood on my ring
finger, the child that always argued

*marriage is a waste of red and diamonds are a waste
of green.* Frightened peers would nervously squeeze

their dolls, tug at the glossy pink ribbon resolving their braids.
I never saw perfection in bows, only restrictions.

How can they expect us to be flawless and oh, so strangled? A
girl in my class brushed my hair
on picture day and I resented

her for years. Now I think of her blonde every time I untangle,
spraying some water to comb out my tongue.

The last word is my favorite one, but I ravel
and twist to see if you'll throttle a brush or

swallow the knot whole.

Calista Ashmore

Follow Me

Backseats covered in scabbed legs and sticky Coke Slurpee

three kids, 97 degrees, one hundred problems, no pennies

couch quarters & dimes get us by—we only need a couple bucks worth of gas to circle a few times

once the lawn chair by the screen door glows amber, we'll know
the check didn't bounce

left turn, left turn, left turn, left turn

our toddlers aren't afraid of the dark anymore

left turn, left turn, left turn, left turn

the rear-view reflects tiny sun-bleached heads bobbing,

Follow me, everything is alright. I'll be the one to tuck you in at night and if you want to leave, I can guarantee, you won't find nobody else like me...

Calista Ashmore

Ranch Recital

On tambourine
shuddering and juddering is the
friendly rattlesnake under the house

dogs in the yard
relentlessly running for jackrabbits
their rowdy and clamorous collars clinking
are my cowbells

for drums
the tireless screen door
nearly thumping off its hinges

a manual F250
my bass player
for nothing tears and roars quite like
that white, dusty ol' faithful

the rooftop weathercock
better known as my electric guitar
twirls to strike the note
right out of thin air

grazing cattle groan in the distance
every great performance
requires backup vocals

I, of course, am the lead singer
yellow wood grass erupts
into applause
a golden ovation

pinching my eyes shut

Calista Ashmore

I fold over
pretending the porch is a platform
that the glochids
at my toes
are roses

The First Time I Saw My Father Cry

The year was 2005
mine was 6
we lived among the rangers and the saints

it was before I understood
the precipitation of people
the overcast in their eyes
Noah's Ark in my neighborhood

until an afternoon in the kitchen
awaiting direction from my imagination
I wandered the motel hall
stopping at a door left ajar

uncovering my father
knees to chest, forehead to foot of bed
two full fists of hair
rocking like that old porch chair

it's the moment I first felt lightning
in my nervous system
the second I was first paralyzed
by thunder shaking the ground

how would I comfort my consolator?
give as his middle taker?
cease his downpour?

that day storms weren't so sinister anymore—
I began to lay on my back in the parking lot
being soaked by the spitter, reaching up and
letting the sky lick my fingers

Calista Ashmore

the year was 2005
mine was 6
the first time I saw my father cry
and understood the flood

Star-Crossed

       Gaping vault above
  cluttered   the soot that
        built   our bones

    Too quiet   We needed more

Forgetting to look down   for the sake of

          sensualizing

  The entire world tethered to bare feet

 Mama's meals sprinkled with   heed
      We   wanted to taste

        more

      gaze up!

    peek down.
       wander
           through…

  existence   devours   Us
     all the   same
 even if   savored from   a
       plastic
                 spoon

Calista Ashmore

Of Your Jaguar Mouth

From Sandra Cisneros

keep it dry as mesquite
snarl smokey nothings

cover your fangs with my mood
leave teeth marks on my shell casings

brass chews better than gold
on a patient tongue

let's savor each other tonight
to again hunt one another come dawn

Calista Ashmore

When My Mother Became a Grandmother

I admired her as she cradled and soothed
cries that used to come from her womb

she touched noses with her heritage and
spoke soft words repeatedly
hoping *I love you* would echo back from
day old lips

a quarter-inch finger twirled her bleached hair
around and around like a carousel
a merry-go-round she could never dizzy on

the apples of her cheeks only perk into
a lasting orb on Christmas
my brother has created her new favorite holiday

she started taking the dogs on long walks
corking the wine bottle before depletion
making chicken salad for lunch

and growing her hair out
long and then even longer
always having plenty of herself to offer
for lengthening fingers to tug

Calista Ashmore

My Iridescent Daggers

Oh, To Be a Maiden

She picks from an orange tree
on the outskirts of Georgia
never intending on
leaving a freshwater tip
the selflessness of the tree
alludes her but
follows her home

She picks from a cherry tree
on the coast of Oregon
until her fingers leave
a crimson touch
she grabs a handful
of stark white cotton
dress anyway
skipping back home

She picks from a lemon tree
in the hills of Texas
plucking sunshine from her giver
pinching seeds with her teeth
puckering her lips
sour and sweet
all the way home

She is watering her solitude
honoring her direction and
her imagination
while the trees wait

Calista Ashmore

never denying grace nor patience
for her to return and replenish
who she once was

My Iridescent Daggers

Christian

You are the space where turbulence turns to silk.
Together we are effortless pandemonium.

Twins separated only by time but
when has time ever been trustworthy?

Spring and summer both bring reminders of fragility with
peeled and bubbled shoulders, war paint freckles.

The blue in your eyes storms mine. The green of me, the magnetism
that attracts women like I to those emerald specks that promise

the protection of nature. They never understand how this hierarchy works.
I am the barrier; you are the cavalry.

You are the sword; I am the shield.
Once you began to correctly pronounce your R's and

your stutter disappeared, they waited for your flag
to skewer sand. The predicament still stands,

fixing is not why you're here, there's no room on deck to
introduce pirates dressed as sailors. Fighting is not the reason

I carved your name on the handle of a jewel covered saber.
Together we are
unchallenging anxiety, getting slipped away like papery cloud cover.

You are the space where choppy waters hush.

Calista Ashmore

I scour the ocean for your lent indigo sight whilst

the lands are dug up by your hands
searching for the leaves of fern I planted
for only you to find.

Branded by an Indian Paintbrush

A five o'clock shadow
scrubbed my face
    I giggled at the sound of threadbare
    and the tickle of love
He always made sure his nuzzling
    never burned and never stung
    a gentle promise of protection
    laced with silver stubble

Each scratch left a pinch of pink
    a gulp of comfort
I am eternally branded by his Indian Paintbrush
    better than a sunset in a child's palms
    I am attached to his roots
    the reason for my stature

Now he calls me *wildflower*
    celebrating my fields every spring
    reminiscing the days before
    I faded to carmine

Calista Ashmore

86

Never do they warn of the ache that follows the mourn. Sexagenarian love, while taking its final gasp, looks and laughs. I'm caught by the hospice nurse reflexively pouring you a glass of wine at 6 o'clock. Now, a photo of you in the passenger seat will have to suffice. Our mattress was sold, a king is too vacant. *Jeopardy!* comes on, I yell out for you from the other room. My rasp echoes back. The house is too big. Speaking about you as if you remain in the recliner beside me, I patiently wait for your mud-covered boots by the screen door to again disappear. I overpay bands on dive bar stages to play *Luckenbach, Texas* by Willie and Waylon; always to remember the warmth of your hands as we swayed. But that's why I said *I do* again and again. The ache that follows the mourn will never be as beautifully blue as the borrowed brooch I wore that May morning we wed.

Calista Ashmore

Forgiveness Trickery

It's spilled salt
seven years of thumbtacks
falling out of the wall

I left the state
it crawled into the
back of my U-Haul

I fled the country
it wedged itself between
my ankle and sock

It's the bird on the fence
staying in the north
disrupting the flock

It's the wet match that won't strike
the new bulb that won't light

It's the *but* that follows *I'm sorry*
it's the forever that forgot always

It's a peace offering unopened
a veil snagged on rose thorns
an entrance for the trojan horse

If you forgive yourself
in the mirror
three times with
your fingers crossed

You will wake
with a dreamcatcher

Calista Ashmore

strapped to your chest

a lullaby pinned to your head

Praying From a Sailboat, Maine

I gripped my fingers
around the rope
pretended we were not
on the ocean or
in the Northeast
I pulled the braid
down to my knees with
a pinch of my accessible force
Dandy, please show me the light of day

The sails rose like a
satiated butterfly would
from a hydrangea bush,
the fog lasted while I was
drowning in my head—

a sunken ship nobody on board could see or hear
then I smiled and the sky flirted
and the sails waved

they waved and waved
and they waved like a practicing toddler
or an angel sitting by a hospital bed

Calista Ashmore

Growing Pains

                      dad said. Angry, enlarged
tumor tugged
            my tendons, shape of a shark tooth. The
pain in his eyes
once he heard the news of my future surgery
                      was my first
time under the knife
now I think of him every time it rains
        I ache, I ache more
    needing to hear his voice on the
phone.
    The growing pains never ceased, dad.

They're not supposed to, kid...

                We will worry when they do.

Calista Ashmore

I Left the Light On

"Sometimes the memory of someone is better than the reality of them."
- Steve Maraboli

I left the light on for you
all   this   time
orange glow has
rotted my porch swing
heart to the nail pierced core
your neglect like termites
ate away relentlessly
chew, chew, chew
flesh and bones
I still waited patiently
there's now a family
of opossums
they hiss and steal
and complain of the rain—
they remind me of you
shadows I know are present
but rarely do they
appear
I wanted the company
needed it even
but still you,
an anachronism

refused

Calista Ashmore

                    I turned the light off

                  you blew in on my stoop
                    I *neglected you* but
                    the bulb went dark
                    as it so often does
                    you know how to
                    hit it where it hurts
                      spew, spew, spew
         my secrets and insecurities
                        clipped onto
                           your belt
          keys to your endless excuse
                    I turned the light off
                      because I knew if
                          I had not
you would have never returned
                  how dare you flare up
                        just to claim
                      me the deserter
                    It appears you forgot
                    I left the light on
                           for you

                      I wish I had not

Fifteen

Venus, strapped in ballet

slippers attempts the worm

on high green carpet

Orion kisses her with

a whip of his belt

Aphrodite invades a

loveseat to bat eyes for

a pomegranate stick-and-poke

from Warhol on her shin

now we're stressed out

I offer Xipe a Lucky Strike

he slaps a butterfly sticker over

the white of my lighter

Jimi thrums an air guitar

pausing only to hand me Visine

I have nothing but

a little skunk to my name

Gods call me *roadkill*

So, You Think You're a Black Kettle?

Buzzin' bee in my bonnet
I wish I could clip their horns but
they always giggle when called *chisel*

I'm trying to burn the breeze out of
this mess. I don't want to be madder than
an old wet hen from yet another

flannel mouth or caterwauling
ten-cent man standing
on a stage in his best bib and tucker
hanging his pick-pocketed fire

Hell, I'm just barkin' at a knot
while they give us a lick and a promise
you know they're all pots, they're all pots.

Calista Ashmore

Castell, Texas

I savored the smoke that escaped your lungs
treating it as if pixie dust was real
the desire to inhale you
to become magic myself

You savored the stench of burnt wood
lingering in my hair
it reminds you of the mountains
you desire to become one
to be at peace yourself

They claim magic is illusory
peace is often mistaken
for paralysis
but I promise that every evening
I will remind you to breathe
if you let me peek up your sleeve

Calista Ashmore

This Is the Last Poem I Write About You

My manuscript's lacuna had your name
in white ink along the margins

the dichotomy of what to say and what to write
while wishing to discontinue the feeling of

letting your voice slip through the cracks of
                memory
tumbling into the void of my confessions

all above board but crystallized with doubt
and as I write your name in oil I recognize

it's a dog that won't hunt here in my house
on this page, in my room, with my new name

My face may be swollen and blue
                but even the sun and the moon
pity your predictable trajectory

I want to air out my lungs but the wind
fetching the past has knocked itself out of me

my future is above snakes but
yours became buzzard food two stanzas ago

Calista Ashmore

Lay Your Head Where You Forget Your Fear

    There's a box that sleeps on my nightstand, a shrine of former friends and naive versions of myself. Concert tickets, polaroids, letters, birthday cards, half heart necklaces. I open it at odd hours, reminiscing with Pandora.
    There's a sanctuary. It fits only tense shoulders and a cloudy head, the hollow nook of a horse's leg. Even on my worst days she matches her heartbeat to mine. We close our eyes to challenge the flies, pounding in unison.
    There's a memorial resting on my lover's sternum. I comb my fingers through his curly, coarse chest hair and pretend I'm weeding away every argument, every ache, every mess. When I wake to walnut brown half circles on my pillowcase, I balance them on my fingertips and blow them into the light of dawn.

Calista Ashmore

Witness

There's a knock on the door, my generation hides
when we set our stories side by side of
ignoring the doorbell and closing the blinds
nobody can conjure up a decent reason as to why

I know that when I hear that wooden thump or echoed ring
the fear is Jehovah himself will be hiding in my burning bushes
floating into my foyer, blowing out my birthday candles to
restrain me with a ratio and mutter what I already figured

God made you by accident, child.

Calista Ashmore

Stained

Stark white, crusty blobs of paint cover my journal
he was using acrylic to write a love letter
that's the kind of poetry I wish dwelled here

Taco Tuesday in our living room
him drawing outside the lines in
ways I could never find the words write

Calista Ashmore

Sisters, Not Twins

after Major Jackson

Our knees ache as we lean down to pick up the pieces
    A grail to assemble our next self

Calista keeps her wrist razor straight as she travels a flat rock
across the shoreline approaching caps

I sit in damp sand guessing how long and how it must feel as
    Earth's thumbprint takes a slow sink

She's covered in truck bed fingernail marks, backseat love
wounds
    My bloody cuticles catch the moth-bitten hem
of my hand-me-down sweater

She prefers to build up the fire
    I insist on babysitting it

We fight over men some days but it's all smoke
    at the end of us

Calista is a professional gambler and I
     violently blush a raspberry flush at my own
intentions

While I tape my mouth with regret-colored ivy
    she climbs vegetation walls and fences

We take a swim in the sticky hot salt, she floats
    her chin above the water but I–

I join a planet coin on the ocean floor

Calista Ashmore

        then swim in erratic panic for the shore

        Life is a game that Calista and I play
so calculated   so afraid   so well

The Third Parent & The Middle Child

Tackle box, swishing with Ozarka and your best big brother jokes. High-pitched comebacks weigh down my pockets. Long Cut Copenhagen takes a few days out of yours. An old burned CD plays Drop the World by Lil Wayne. We know every word. We don't hook anything, not at first. I laugh at all your jokes—

your smirking dip lip. The CD scratches. Then it skips. You cast another line. I do too. You reek of bass. I wreak havoc. And that's how we've always done it. I raise Hell. You ice it. I wander. You search. I scream. You shush.

I drop the world. You pick it up for me.

Calista Ashmore

Has Anybody Seen Mary Margaret?

There, beyond the Sandia's, have you seen
her pouring propane into a burner?

Over in Urbandale being frugal, burying
bottles in the backyard broadleaf milkweed?

She was last photographed in the winter of '79
lowering her husband into Fairview

her shovel barely pierced the crust
of the limestone Permian Basin

I'm sure she's collecting tissues
into her carpet bag and begging the captain to

leave the cabin light on until
she lands a new life in dicty Dallas

and there she will leave unsolved puzzles
sprawled across the kitchen counter

they didn't provide a hint for why
cold, calloused hands are crawling up her

stocking covered thighs as she pours the
window seat a Jack Daniel's.

I saw Mary Margaret last night as I walked down the aisle,

eyes as wide and Cerrillos turquoise as ever
her salt and pepper feathers soared through the pines

Calista Ashmore

with her new wings I wonder if anybody has seen Mary
Margaret skyward

since the puzzles have vanished into the drawers &
her rusted garden tools boast undisturbed dust

LANDMAN

James broke his back on a diamond plate staircase in Anderson. He got a check. Nobody checked in.

Bill's heart went out with a light beer in his hands in Midland. His dad found him & still spends his half-hour breaks in that double-wide every day.

Mitchell lost his left-hand fingertips to a hitch ball. He was fired for the mistake. Now he has a fancy tech job in Charlotte.

Bryson was burned alive. So was Matt. So was Bradley. So was Jason. They were all kind & they were all cremated.

The rig wives don't sleep at night and the voiceless house is smothered with steel toe ghosts. Bone dry crumbs in bold
    on vinyl plank–

            There's no water left in this town. Blood is thinner than oil.

Calista Ashmore

Belonging

October will soon perish
wishing not to bloom
autumn allows spring to spring
and spring allows autumn to shed
together they belong
wearing yellow patience
and russet, shedding
to spring yet again

If you are summer
do not try to be winter
it is busy freezing
you, summer, must go melt
your day will always approach
in time, you, wearing
crimson and gold
shall scorn

Calista Ashmore

I'm Planting

As a child I believed I would grow a watermelon in my belly if I ingested the seeds. I spent hours under the Texas sun, cornered in a wobbly plastic chair by the pool, plucking the culprit with the far-left fork tine.

As a teen I believed if I let someone know me well enough, I would form embers of love so strong it would burn us both until we spread apart, cold as ash. I spent hours, crouched on a green plaid couch, cornered by standing legs of loud party goers and conversing friends, hugging my knees while my internal voice practiced pronouncing my alias.

That's the thing about growing into each year of life. You are met with moments where you feel silly and outsmarted, you finally let yourself plant seeds of watermelon in your body and stretch your legs into a new friendship and move toward the middle of the room, because you will be okay. You know now, the liberation of fruit, the mirror carved in a crystal ashtray.

Calista Ashmore

Del Rio

Five miles from Black Brush to border

    hidden eyes
in shrubs and behind trees
    dirty white t-shirts
bloody knees

    hide water bottles in the rosette leaves
nourish the breathing creosote bushes—
Seen anything suspicious?

    No, Sir, nothing strange to me

Calista Ashmore

He Can Always Hear Me

To Aaron

I sing in showers of vacant rooms
he somehow belts along
never missing a beat of my tenderness

He hums my hymns in his sleep
his chest rises and falls
an instrument only him and I can tune

The lyrics echo the halls of our home
walls lit with framed love letters
pillowcases scented with lavender and laughter

The record stings then spins
we follow suit
our midnights here are never quiet

The wolves are in the yard, begging the moon
he's downstairs churning his neck upward
reverberating his roar mouthed muse

Calista Ashmore

Morning Melody

Conversationalists, dining over plates of ivy
           dayspring light streams into your espresso eyes

crepe myrtles shed cotton candy outside the window yet
        at you, I continue to gaze

the doors are open as you April the lawn
        & I *A-side or B-side* with lace fingers

the weatherman warns of a severely sunny Sunday
           you beamed so brilliantly; I eclipsed my poppy
cheeks under straw

our toes tangle beneath linen, our maple-leaf lips drip sugar
down our chins,
           bookcases silently crawl up the white smoke
    walls

how intoxicating it is—there's no leather-bound backbone
          embracing a love poem quite like ours

Calista Ashmore

My Iridescent Daggers

I Met Calista on a Park Bench

She sat beside me in an ivory sundress

unbothered by the consequences
that were the bench's bird blemishes

I crossed my legs with her bravery
as an obsessed apprentice

a love letter from her parents
nodded in her fist

she spoke in spiders
every sentence having many legs—

recounting each person who wished
to wrap her convictions in a paper towel

and discard them in the backyard.
She giggled a confession,

I always crawled
back into the house

her gloriously timeless resilience,
a sentiment of relentless progress…

I stagger and stutter in my awe

the sky's curtain then opened
her first act was to lift her dress

stroke her long blonde thigh hair
a cohesive choreography of fair Rockettes

ungroomed but well-kept
just how she likes it

a soft but unwavering voice
promised shade for sunburnt places

cradled my envy in its arms
I responded only with nervous salutations

afraid she would hear my desires tremble
or smell nicotine on my breath

with every deep exhale I could feel
kindness, comfort, solace, sympathy

her pearls did not rattle
unless reassuring

my first prayer in months
clamored internally

a plea that reincarnation is real
if I could not be her then

I would be something very close.
Stretching into departure

a refusal to break eye contact
immobilized me

Just wait, honey, you'll see
her pearls a bouncing pair of die

years later I met

My Iridescent Daggers

her emeralds in the mirror

she smirked, cocked her eyebrow
like a proud professor

as if to say
I told you so

as if to say without
saying anything at all

      just how we like it.

Calista Ashmore

Good Luck

Kiss me & throw me back

I am something you parade
stifling me with both slimy hands
but never will I win a spot on
your wall for a chance to sing & dance

I prefer the depths of salted darkness
breathing in buttered teal seafoam
unlearning that shining silver slits gold gills
not much of a catch but a catch

nonetheless so please pry open
my pharynx with your fingers,
release me from your small sickle then

Kiss me & throw me back

Calista Ashmore

Nana's Chocolate Fudge (Serves You Right)

1 cup of *Bless Your Heart*
2 tablespoons of cayenne pepper for spice
1 bag of overly ripened apologies
3 tablespoons of granulated regret
12 fluid ounces of Whoop Ass
Half a gallon of nerve
Add respect to taste
Garnish with the stems of creativity
Serve hot and unbothered

Calista Ashmore

68

I glance in the mirror, and you know,
it's uncertain
            if my eyes have blued
from aging or watching my
children grow up
& my parents
die off

my forehead looks itself like a grave
and my teeth are browning at the edges
the time passed so fast all I got was
the smothering pop of a backfire
billowing from a suited up 2010 hearse
        now I call my granddaughter *baby girl*
she gazes up with eyes a different shade
than mine
        —ocean green

my pocket knife is dull from etching inches
into the knotted basement oak panels
all my socks have frayed holes
from wiggling toes
trying to stay standing while
burying a best friend

each year the cake is cluttered with
candles so close together
I get claustrophobic

I left the cups cupboard open again
and my mug sweating
onto the countertop half-full

Calista Ashmore

each year the race ends but
I never hear the piercing start whistle
now my wife is decorating our 35th Christmas tree

The moon travels at 2,200 miles per hour
and my God do I know how exhausting
it is to come and to go

The First Time I Heard My Mother Cry

The day I left for Texas lil man told me he saw her tear up but
by
the time I got inside she replaced the rumor with that sweet,
pure grin on her face. Our dog was dyin' and I was feldgin' but
still she beamed. Mama never even got close to cryin'. Her
daddy left her for the wide blue yonder at nine and I think that
must have been the last time, somethin' like 1979. She just
holds it in, I guess.
All them tears get soaked up by wine and bakers twine and
needing to be stronger than
anybody else in the room. She told me hallooin' is good for ya
but showed me that
hootin' might as well be a crime. Gotta be a tough broad
because who's gonna take care of you?
Two days before I got married, she buzzed my pocket full of
dandelions. *Well, honey, I finally got her RSVP.* The way her
voice croaked against my cheek stung so bad I thought I was
struck by a BB gun by one of the cousins again.
The year was 2024, mine was 25, the first time I heard my
mother cry, finally finishing the drought.

Calista Ashmore

Acknowledgements

I'd like to thank some of the organizations and individuals who offered me guidance, acceptance, and care through this process. I am eternally grateful.

The Writers' League of Texas

Aspen Summer Words

New Orleans Poetry Festival

San Miguel International Literary Festival

Mentors Major Jackson, Anna Scotti, Abe Louise Young, & Judyth Hill

To my colleagues & friends of the Westbank Library Community District

To my dear friends Rachel, Vikram, Skylar, Maureen, Emily, Jessica, Liz, Erin, and Sam for your edits and honest feedback

To my incredible family, especially my parents and grandparents, for letting me share these stories in my abstract perspective

To my husband. Aaron, you are my daily reminder that art is everywhere. Our life together will always be my favorite poem.

Calista Ashmore

My Iridescent Daggers

Thank you.

With all my love and daggers,
Calista.

www.ingramcontent.com/pod-product-compliance
Lightning Source LLC
Chambersburg PA
CBHW022057120526
44580CB00013B/39